FREEDOM FROM DEBT

Biblical Keys to Financial Abundance

CHRIST
FOR ALL NATIONS

Australia • Brazil • Canada • Germany • Hong Kong • Singapore
South Africa • United Kingdom • United States

Freedom from Debt - Biblical Keys to Financial Abundance

© 2017, CfaN Christ for all Nations

Published by Christ for all Nations
P.O. Box 590585
Orlando, Florida 32859 U.S.A.
www.cfan.org

Editorial by Leslyn Musch
Layout Design Grupo Nivel Uno, Inc

Unless otherwise indicated, all Scripture quotations are taken from
the New King James Version of the Bible. Copyright © 1982,
Thomas Nelson, Inc., Publishers

The Holy Bible: New Living Translation. Carol Stream, IL: Tyndale House Publishers (2013).

The Holy Bible: New International Version. Grand Rapids, MI: Zondervan (1984).

ISBN: 978-1-933446-56-1

Printed in the United States of America

INTRODUCTION

by DANIEL KOLENDA

I was living by faith as a Bible college student. The end of one semester had arrived, and I faced the deadline to pay my bills to enroll for the next semester. I needed $2,000 by the end of the day. But I only had $200 in my bank account. I was in my dorm room praying. *Lord, you promised that you would provide for my needs. I need your provision today.* I felt the Lord speak to my heart reminding me of words I had heard somewhere before. "If what you have in your hand will not meet your need, it can't be your harvest. It must be your seed." It occurred to me that the $200 in my account was the tithe of the $2000 I needed for school. Isn't it amazing that, as 2 Corinthians 9:10 says, God even provides the seed for the sower!

I knew what the Lord was asking me to do. He wanted me to trust Him. *Lord where should I give my seed?* Just then, there was a knock at the door. When I opened, one of my classmates stood there with tears in his eyes. "I've come to say goodbye," he said. That day was the deadline for the deposit on his dorm room, and he did not have enough. "How much do you need?" I asked. He said, "I need $300, but I only have $100." "I have the other $200 for you," I said with joy. I wrote the check and gave it to him. I shut the door, got back on my knees and prayed again. *Well Lord, I've cleared out my account. Now there is plenty of room for you to bless me,*" I said almost tongue-in-cheek. Later that day I went to the local public library to check my email. A message had arrived from my father. He said that he had received a check in the mail for me. It was from an old family friend who felt led to send it for my school expenses. It more than covered the $2000 I needed.

That was one of the first times I experienced a financial miracle. Although today I often face financial needs in the millions of dollars, the principles I learned as a Bible college student still hold true. The Holy Spirit was teaching me that Jesus wants to be Lord over every area of my life – including my finances. But this is not because He needs my resources; it is because I need His. He wants my life to be blessed, and whatever is put into His hands is blessed abundantly! Reinhard Bonnke told me that the Lord once spoke to him saying, "For every deadline I will throw you a lifeline." Yet God's "lifelines" often look like risks. He asks us to surrender what is ours so we can receive what is His.

First Kings 17 tells the story of how ravens fed Elijah by the Kerith Brook during a severe famine. After the brook dried up, the Lord spoke to Elijah: "Go and live in the village of Zarephath, near the city of Sidon. I have instructed a widow there to feed you" (1 King 17:9 NLT). On the surface, this verse sounds like God sends Elijah to the widow so she can take care of him. But that doesn't make sense. Widows in the ancient world were usually poor and destitute – all the more during a famine.

God could have sent Elijah to the richest man in Israel. For that matter, God could have continued to feed him supernaturally as He had been doing. Why then would God send his hungry prophet to a woman with the least to give? There is only one possible answer. God didn't send Elijah to the widow to provide for Elijah. God sent Elijah to the widow to provide for the widow. But notice how the miracle God wanted to perform for the widow was contingent on an act of obedience and trust. Her "lifeline" looked more like a noose to natural eyes. She had to give her last bit of flour and oil to Elijah before using it for herself and her son. Yet her willingness to obey and trust God opened a fountain of blessing that she could never have imagined! If you want your finances to be blessed, the Lord will ask you to put them into His hand. He wants to be the Lord over every area of your life because He wants every area of your life to flourish.

Money is not just about "money." It represents an area in our hearts that has deep significance. God wants to rule that area like every other. Sometimes we separate finances from life in God's Kingdom. We may not say it that way, but it's often implied by the way we operate. We either make finances too central in our focus (as a point of worry or lust), or a taboo issue we are afraid to address. But Jesus did neither. He boldly taught disciples that a major part of their lives was the way they related to money. Stewardship of our finances reflects the depths of our heart, and influences the world for eternity. It is a major issue. That is why we must give Jesus full dominion of that area of our lives.

Jesus, Be Lord of All

As a missionary evangelist, God has given me the privilege to preach the gospel throughout Africa and around the world. No matter where I go or what crowd is before me, the basic content of my message is always the same – Jesus.

"There is no other name under heaven given to mankind by which we must be saved" (Acts 4:12b NIV). Christ Himself is the centerpiece and substance of the message I preach. His blood purchases salvation.

His name drives out demons. His presence heals the sick. And His goodness draws the needy into His loving arms. Our gospel is not another religious philosophy; it is not a sales pitch. It is the revelation of a Man – *the* Man, Christ Jesus.

Faith with repentance is the only fitting response to such a message. For this gospel unveils Jesus as the glorious Sovereign, the King and Lord over all creation, every nation and each person. So when people respond, they must make Jesus Lord of their lives. Every area of the human heart becomes subject to His divine rule. That is what the "Kingdom" of God is all about – submitting completely to King Jesus. But this submission does not end once we get saved. It *begins* once we get saved. From that day forward Jesus' rule constantly increases over every area of our lives like the dawning sun rises steadily to transform night into day.

The Gospel is not just about getting to Heaven – it's about getting Heaven into us and through us to the world around us. The Gospel is relevant to every area of life and the more we recognize that, the more we see the dominion of God (the Kingdom of Heaven) touching and redeeming even the most ordinary things.

Redeeming the Time

In I Peter 1:18-19 NIV we read, "For you know that it was not with perishable things such as silver or gold that you were redeemed from the empty way of life handed down to you from your ancestors, but with the precious blood of Christ, a lamb without blemish or defect."

I often preach about the blood of Jesus as God's remedy for sin. I talk about its power to redeem our souls and break every chain. Yet notice where this verse puts its focus. It does not emphasize how we were redeemed from sin by the blood of Jesus. Nor does it stress how we were redeemed from demonic bondages by the blood of Jesus (though these things are certainly true). But this verse specifically declares that we were redeemed from *"the empty way of life"* we inherited from our forefathers. In other words, the blood of Jesus saves us from a worthless life!

Paul explains further: "See then that you walk circumspectly, not as fools but as wise, redeeming the time, because the days are evil" (Eph 5:15-16).

I remember when I was young, adults often quoted this verse to encourage me not to waste time. I was told to "redeem the time" by using my time wisely. But Scripture speaks here of something far more profound than time management.

Time is a destroyer. People throughout history have recognized this unfortunate reality. Many pagan religions have gods to represent time and they are often pictured as destructive and even frightening monsters. Hinduism for example has the goddess Kali who is usually pictured wearing a necklace of decapitated heads and a skirt of dismembered arms. She brandishes a blood-soaked sword and stands on the bodies of slain victims. She is considered the embodiment of time which devours everything. In Greek mythology, Kronos, the god of time, devoured his own children. Even in popular culture, "Father Time" is usually depicted with a harvesting scythe similar to the Grim Reaper.

In the modern world we have a more scientific view of the destructive nature of time. In physics, for example, there is the principle of entropy – the idea that every system tends towards chaos over time. Everything breaks down. Everything is moving towards an ever-increasing state of disorder.

Time is not our friend – it is a destroyer. If you have any doubt about that, just look in the mirror. You can see the corrosive effects of time in your own body. As natural as this principle is, there is something about it that feels inexplicably unnatural to us. Ecclesiastes 3:11 says that God has put eternity in the hearts of men. We are beings that were created for eternity. We have an inherent sense that something is terribly wrong in this mortal world. Decay and death are such a routine part of the natural order, and yet we possess a profound hatred for them. We all have the instinct to fight entropy with every fiber of our being. This is why we maintain our bodies, our cars and houses. When we see things breaking down we want to fix them and spend much of our lives doing so.

But our instinct to fight entropy goes far beyond simple maintenance. We have a desire to do something truly meaningful – to create or contribute something to the world that will last forever. People express this in a variety of ways. They might become an environmentalist or some kind of activist. They may write books, design art or build monuments they hope will outlive and immortalize them.

But the truth is that all these temporary memorials we fight to build are pretty meaningless in the grand scheme. In fact, someone could make a good argument that, from a purely natural perspective, there is no way to achieve anything that has true meaning. Even the Bible recognizes this: "Meaningless! Meaningless… Everything is meaningless" (Eccl 1:2 NIV). Without some kind of redemptive intervention, everything will burn. Time will destroy it all. All of our achievements – monuments, books, art, and environmental and humanitarian work – will soon be finished and forgotten. This is why secular thought has tended towards postmodernism and nihilism. For those without Jesus, nothing really matters.

But the redeemed have amazing ability no other creatures possess. We have the power to *live* redemptively – to convert temporary resources, like time and money, into eternal assets. That is how Paul can encourage us to "redeem the time." The blood of Jesus has redeemed us from a worthless life. As a result, we also now have authority to redeem our energy, productivity, intelligence, material, wealth, days and everything else *into eternal value*.

This is why your finances matter so much. You are one of the few creatures in existence that possesses the ability to do something eternal with your resources. What a privilege! And what a responsibility! No wonder Jesus Himself addressed the issue of finances so explicitly.

Redeeming Finances in the Kingdom

A crucial aspect of Jesus' teaching was His disciples' stewardship of their financial resources. We know the verse well, and quote it often. "But seek first the kingdom of God and His righteousness, and all these things shall be added to you" (Matt 6:33). But look carefully at the context. That verse concludes a section of teaching in which Jesus taught His disciples how *to steward their financial resources.* Right in the center of the Sermon on the Mount, Jesus instructs His disciples how to manage their money.

We tend to focus on the promise that God will provide! But that promise rests on the all-important condition that we pursue God's Kingdom above all else. That condition, in fact, is the ultimate Kingdom secret to financial freedom and abundance. When we fulfill that condition, we make Jesus Lord of our wealth and attract God's powerful blessing.

What then does it mean? How do we seek God's Kingdom "first"? Does this mean we pray and read the Bible first thing in the morning, before our coffee and the newspaper? Or does it simply mean that we tithe before spending our income on other things? These are indeed good ways to prioritize God's Kingdom. But Jesus was saying something on a much deeper level. In the broader context of this chapter, Jesus taught *a whole way of life* that put God's Kingdom first by the way we steward our resources.

This section began with a teaching about money – specifically, about giving to the poor (Matt 6:1-4). Jesus told His disciples that they should do so "in secret," not for religious display. Giving offerings simply to look pious might impress people, but it surely does not impress God. He will offer no reward for such vain sacrifices. God desires the secret sacrifices that only He can see. That is true giving, a genuine act of love and worship. It's done from the heart, rather than out of obligation or pretense.

But Jesus was not merely teaching us how to give with integrity. He was teaching us how to steward our resources for supernatural results. Secret giving purifies our character, but it also maximizes our investment. Take a closer look at Jesus' words. "But when you give to the poor, do not let your left hand know what your right hand is doing, so that your giving will be in secret; and your Father who sees what is done in secret will reward you" (Matt 6:3-4 NASB). Did you catch that last phrase? The Father "will reward you." He does not only see what we give in secret; He *rewards* what we give in secret.

The Greek word for "reward" can also mean, "to give back, pay back, or fulfill an obligation." Jesus used it here to say, "When you make investments into God's Kingdom out of pure compassion, faith and sincerity, He will return eternal increase to your account." Christians often read this passage and walk away with only one part of the lesson: that we should give with integrity. Yet Jesus gives us at least two points here. First, our giving should be in secret. And second: *God will reward us*.

Jesus goes on to teach on prayer and fasting in the exact same way. All three spiritual disciplines – giving to the poor, praying and fasting – are ways we invest in God's Kingdom. All three receive rewards. The way we manage our finances is just as important as the way we manage prayer and fasting! In fact, out of the three, Jesus taught about giving first. Stewarding our money the Kingdom way is just as important as the other disciplines – the ones we usually deem more "spiritual." But our financial life is not in a separate category. It is an integral part of our one devotional life. It is an integral part of living in God's Kingdom, under Jesus' lordship.

The Church must adopt this integrated, "Kingdom" mindset if we want God to liberate us from debt and bless us with abundance. That is why Jesus returned to the topic of financial stewardship right after He taught on fasting. In reality, He never left the subject of stewardship. Finances just reveal our faithful management the most clearly. So He went on to say, "Do not store up for yourselves treasures on earth, where moth and rust destroy, and where thieves break in and steal. But store up for yourselves treasures in heaven, where neither moth nor rust destroys, and where thieves do not break in or steal; for where your treasure is, there your heart will be also" (Matt 6:19-21 NASB).

These are powerful words about financial stewardship, foundational to everything else the Bible teaches about wealth. I believe Christians often read these words through the wrong lens and miss their vast implications. But let's try to take Jesus at His Word. Read those versus again. Notice how Jesus did not teach His disciples to avoid money. The issue of wealth will always be a part of life in God's Kingdom. So Jesus taught His disciples how to master it, by making wise investments versus foolish ones

Jesus even played on our desire for wealth. He never said, "If you are truly spiritual and desire my Kingdom, you will not desire treasure." No, He said, "Where your treasure *is,* there your hearts will be also." It is therefore not sinful to desire wealth. Rather it is sinful to desire the wrong *kind* of wealth, or to desire it for the wrong reasons. Otherwise, Jesus could not have commanded us to store up treasures *for ourselves.*

Remember, money is more than a necessary tool. It is also God's wonderful gift for us to use for His purposes. When we pursue wealth for ourselves, we make it an idol and stop serving God. "You cannot serve God and mammon" (Matt 6:24). But when we make Jesus Lord of our finances, managing our physical resources according to Kingdom principles, we become wealthy in the truest sense of that term. God will provide for our needs and bless us with abundance for others. That blessing enables us to help people in need, live free from debt and anxiety, and store up wealth in an eternal storeroom.

This is exactly what Jesus meant when He said, "Seek first God's Kingdom." Our Lord was instructing us to manage all of our resources – our finances, energy, time and bodies – in ways that advanced His cause rather than ours. If we adopt that lifestyle, then Jesus promised that God would touch our finances – and our whole lives – with abundance. Or as He put it, "All these things will be added to you." One day we will discover that all along we have been investing in an eternally secure depository. Our treasures will be great in the age to come. It's the perfect retirement plan.

The Financial Potential of Christians

Among all the people in the world, Christians should be the most effective at making and using money. I am not saying all Christians should be wealthy by the world's standards. There may be times we go through trials or God calls us to make sacrifices. Sometimes Christians suffer financially because of their faith. Recently in the USA, several followers of Jesus have lost their businesses and sustained lawsuits because of their convictions. The apostle Paul felt the full spectrum of financial situations. He knew what it was like to go through seasons of "abundance and suffering need" (Phil 4:12 NASB).

But then he also said, "I can do all things through Him who strengthens me" (Phil 4:13 NASB). There is a powerful secret in those words. Even during lean times, the God to whom Paul fervently prayed *always* provided. He would always enable Paul to bless others. The great apostle had "learned the secret" of how never to be in lack no matter the situation. Financial "abundance" and "strength" do not always require Christians to have tremendous wealth at our disposal. Under God's mighty touch, we have the ability to bless others even during difficult times.

So believers should lead the way in financial wisdom and prosperity. We operate in our Father's favor and power. His Word gives us potent insight, and promises financial blessing to those who walk in His ways. There should be no group of people who are more successful, creative and generous in their use of money than followers of Jesus Christ.

But this is often not the case, and Jesus recognized that disparity. He told His disciples that the people of the world are often wiser in their stewardship than those in His Kingdom (Luke 16:8). Jesus even used a dishonest business manager to make His point. Even though the manager was unrighteous and wasted his master's money, he still understood his God-given potential to use money for his future advantage. He had no integrity. But at least he had the sense and creativity to use wealth as a powerful tool for a higher purpose – even if that purpose was selfish. How much more, Jesus said, should *His* people use money in the same way, but for God's righteous purposes.

"I tell you, make friends for yourselves using worldly riches so that when those riches are gone, you will be welcomed in those homes that continue forever" (Luke 16:9 NCV). In other words, Jesus tells us to invest temporal wealth into God's eternal purposes. How remarkable! Even though the world's money cannot *purchase* eternal things (1 Pet 1:18-19), we can still *use* the world's money for Kingdom purposes. Such usage will then yield eternal dividends for us in the coming age. What greater investment could there be? According to Jesus in the story of the unrighteous steward, we actually can take the financial resources of this world – the same wealth sometimes used on earth for wicked purposes – and *redeem it for eternal purposes!*

So if that is true, shouldn't Christians be the very best at using money? Shouldn't we work the hardest, be the most generous and invest our money with the greatest wisdom – the wisdom of eternity? Yet some Christians disregard this powerful tool out of some kind of false spirituality. They feel they can avoid hard work because they are "trusting God," or they can disregard God's holy purpose for finances because of all the "greedy preachers on TV." Yet these are really just excuses.

Jesus was right. "The people of this world are often shrewder in dealing with their own kind than are the people of the light" (Luke 16:8 NVI). But He gives us hope in that same story. "I say to you, make friends for yourselves by means of the wealth of unrighteousness, so that when it fails, they will receive you into the eternal dwellings" (Luke 16:9 NASB).

We can learn our identity as Christian stewards and begin to fulfill our potential. If we choose to adopt the King's ways, we can become more prudent than the world with our finances. God's wisdom is available to us. He offers us His wisdom, as well as His blessing. We can walk faithfully in His ways and He will empower us to prosper for Him. We can invest our resources prudently into the works of God's Kingdom. As disciples of Jesus Christ, it is time to fulfill our potential as "sons of light." It is time for Christians to experience financial freedom and supernatural abundance. Then we would be able to finance God's works around the world and lead the way for others to follow.

This is why God wants us free from debt and blessed financially. It is for His purposes and testimony, not for our selfish interests. Of course, it is wonderful when we enjoy the benefits of God's financial blessings – and there is nothing wrong with this. When water flows through a pipe, the pipe also gets wet as the water travels to its destination. But we must remember that we are not the terminus. God always blesses us so that we can be a blessing in turn. We want to support His purposes in this world, and "train to reign" in the future! Jesus desires the central place in our finances. His Kingdom should rule every part of our lives – including our wealth.

So here is the key to financial freedom and abundance: Make Jesus Lord of your finances. That may sound simple and obvious, but it's actually a profound truth we must hear again on a whole new level. Jesus' lordship unlocks every other promise in Scripture about our wealth. We must deliberately give Him "free reign" as King of our finances. His Kingdom should govern our physical resources, just as it should govern our speech, relationships, thoughts, appetites, time management and devotional lives. How do we do that in our finances? The same way we make Him Lord of these other areas. We surrender all to Him, search the Scriptures for His wisdom, apply that wisdom through obedience, declare His promises and dare to trust Him for everything. He will lead the way out of debt and into financial freedom and abundance.

This booklet will help you do these very things. Rather than offer a systematic study or technical guide for budgeting, we are giving you a treasure trove of biblical passages, principles and promises. We present the raw materials of God's Word to build a financial life that is free of debt and full of abundance. The thirty-one declarations for breakthrough are themselves worth the price of the book. Take this powerful resource and use it to make Jesus Lord of your finances, and to experience His abundance in your life today.

Daniel Kolenda

BIBLICAL KEYS

to Financial Abundance

HOPE FOR YOUR FINANCES

There is good news today for your finances! The Lord wants to speak to you through His Word to encourage you, build your faith and let you know that He is right there to walk with you through whatever you are facing financially. No matter if you are deeply in debt or if you purely want to increase your wealth to further the Kingdom, applying God's promises and principles can lead you out of debt and into financial freedom!

You may be thinking, "but my situation is so bad that financial health is impossible." To you, Jesus says, "With men this is impossible, but with God all things are possible" (Matt 19:26b).

As you dig into the Word of God to uncover treasures of truth in the following pages, the Bible gives you a vital key to positioning your heart and life to receive the abundant blessings of God.

"Now it shall come to pass, if you diligently obey the voice of the LORD your God, to observe carefully all His commandments which I command you today, that the LORD your God will set you high above all nations of the earth. And all these blessings shall come upon you and overtake you, because you obey the voice of the LORD your God" (Deut 28:1-2). Following God's direction in the Bible is key to financial turnaround.

This booklet is neither a "how-to" manual about budgets nor an in-depth study. Rather, it contains a wealth of wisdom from the Word of God. It is filled with God's promises, His principles and His thoughts about your financial wellbeing. God desires to bless you! I invite you to step into His abundance and be transformed by the renewing of your mind through the Word of God.

Promises for Your Finances

"For I know the plans I have for you," declares the Lord, "plans to prosper you and not to harm you, plans to give you hope and a future." **Jer 29:11** NIV

Let them shout for joy and be glad,
Who favor my righteous cause;
And let them say continually,
"Let the Lord be magnified,
Who has pleasure in the prosperity of His servant." **Ps 35:27**

The blessing of the Lord makes one rich,
And He adds no sorrow with it. **Prov 10:22**

Honor the Lord with your possessions,
And with the firstfruits of all your increase;
So your barns will be filled with plenty,
And your vats will overflow with new wine. **Prov 3:9-10**

I will go before you
And make the crooked places straight;
I will break in pieces the gates of bronze
And cut the bars of iron.
I will give you the treasures of darkness
And hidden riches of secret places,
That you may know that I, the Lord,
Who call you by your name,
Am the God of Israel. **Is 45:2-3**

And you shall remember the Lord your God, for it is He who gives you power to get wealth, that He may establish His covenant which He swore to your fathers, as it is this day. **Deut 8:18**

Give, and it will be given to you: good measure, pressed down, shaken together, and running over will be put into your bosom. For with the same measure that you use, it will be measured back to you. **Luke 6:38**

A single day in your courts
is better than a thousand anywhere else!
I would rather be a gatekeeper in the house of my God
than live the good life in the homes of the wicked.
For the Lord God is our sun and our shield.
He gives us grace and glory.
The Lord will withhold no good thing
from those who do what is right.
O Lord of Heaven's Armies,
what joy for those who trust in you. **Ps 84:10-12** NLT

Remember this—a farmer who plants only a few seeds will get a small crop. But the one who plants generously will get a generous crop.

You must each decide in your heart how much to give. And don't give reluctantly or in response to pressure. "For God loves a person who gives cheerfully." And God will generously provide all you need. Then you will always have everything you need and plenty left over to share with others. **2 Cor 9:6-8** NLT

And this same God who takes care of me will supply all your needs from his glorious riches, which have been given to us in Christ Jesus. **Phil 4:19** NLT

Aligning Your Heart for Blessing

Salvation is the greatest blessing you can receive. Every blessing flows from relationship with Jesus. If you have not given your life to Jesus, ask Him to be your Lord and Savior right now. Make today the day of your salvation:
For God says, "At just the right time, I heard you. On the day of salvation, I helped you."
Indeed, the "right time" is now. Today is the day of salvation. **2 Cor 6:2** NLT

For God so loved the world that He gave His only begotten Son, that whoever believes in Him should not perish but have everlasting life. For God did not send His Son into the world to condemn the world, but that the world through Him might be saved. **John 3:16-17**

If you openly declare that Jesus is Lord and believe in your heart that God raised him from the dead, you will be saved. For it is by believing in your heart that you are made right with God, and it is by openly declaring your faith that you are saved. **Rom 10:9-10** NLT

In Christ, all of your spiritual debt is cancelled and wiped away:
When you came to Christ, you were "circumcised," but not by a physical procedure. Christ performed a spiritual circumcision—the

cutting away of your sinful nature. For you were buried with Christ when you were baptized. And with him you were raised to new life because you trusted the mighty power of God, who raised Christ from the dead.

You were dead because of your sins and because your sinful nature was not yet cut away. Then God made you alive with Christ, for he forgave all our sins. He canceled the record of the charges against us and took it away by nailing it to the cross. In this way, he disarmed the spiritual rulers and authorities. He shamed them publicly by his victory over them on the cross. **Col 2:11-15** NLT

Live in awe and reverence of the Lord:
Blessed is every one who fears the Lord,
Who walks in His ways.
When you eat the labor of your hands,
You shall be happy, and it shall be well with you. **Ps 128:1-2**

Like Abraham, you are blessed to be a blessing:
I will make you a great nation;
I will bless you
And make your name great;
And you shall be a blessing.
I will bless those who bless you,
And I will curse him who curses you;
And in you all the families of the earth shall be blessed.
Gen 12:2-3

Live a life of generosity:
Give to him who asks you, and from him who wants to borrow from you do not turn away. **Matt 5:42**

Seek to live your life like Jesus in love and mercy:
But love your enemies, do good, and lend, hoping for nothing in return; and your reward will be great, and you will be sons of the Most High. For He is kind to the unthankful and evil. Therefore be merciful, just as your Father also is merciful. **Luke 6:35-36**

Pursue unity for it commands a blessing:
Behold, how good and how pleasant it is
For brethren to dwell together in unity!
It is like the precious oil upon the head,
Running down on the beard,
The beard of Aaron,
Running down on the edge of his garments.
It is like the dew of Hermon,
Descending upon the mountains of Zion;
For there the Lord commanded the blessing—
Life forevermore. **Ps 133:1-3**

Blessing comes as you trust in the Lord and make Him your hope and confidence:
But blessed are those who trust in the Lord
and have made the Lord their hope and confidence.
They are like trees planted along a riverbank,
with roots that reach deep into the water.
Such trees are not bothered by the heat
or worried by long months of drought.
Their leaves stay green,
and they never stop producing fruit. **Jer 17:7-8** NLT

Getting the Bible's Perspective on Debt

The rich rules over the poor,
And the borrower is servant to the lender. **Prov 22:7**

Work hard and become a leader;
be lazy and become a slave. **Prov 12:24** NLT

Don't agree to guarantee another person's debt
or put up security for someone else.
If you can't pay it,
even your bed will be snatched from under you. **Prov 22:26-27** NLT

The wicked borrows and does not repay,
But the righteous shows mercy and gives. **Ps 37:21**

Let no debt remain outstanding, except the continuing debt to love
one another, for he who loves his fellowman has fulfilled the law.
Rom 13:8 NIV

Don't love money; be satisfied with what you have. For God has said, "I
will never fail you.
I will never abandon you." **Heb 13:5** NLT

You were bought at a price; do not become slaves of men. **I Cor 7:23**

The wise have wealth and luxury,
but fools spend whatever they get. **Prov 21:20** NLT

But people who long to be rich fall into temptation and are trapped
by many foolish and harmful desires that plunge them into ruin and
destruction. For the love of money is the root of all kinds of evil. And

some people, craving money, have wandered from the true faith and pierced themselves with many sorrows. **I Tim 6:9-10** NLT

And He [Jesus] said to them, "Take heed and beware of covetousness, for one's life does not consist in the abundance of the things he possesses." **Luke 12:15**

Breaking the Cycle of Debt

Submit yourself to the Lordship of Jesus Christ:
No one can serve two masters. For you will hate one and love the other; you will be devoted to one and despise the other. You cannot serve both God and money. **Matt 6:24** NLT

Commit yourself to be a person of integrity:
By this I know that You are well pleased with me,
Because my enemy does not triumph over me.
As for me, You uphold me in my integrity,
And set me before Your face forever. **Ps 41:11-12**

Give yourself to study the Bible so that you will know how to live according to God's ways:
This Book of the Law shall not depart from your mouth, but you shall meditate in it day and night, that you may observe to do according to all that is written in it. For then you will make your way prosperous, and then you will have good success. **Josh 1:8**

Diligently and faithfully work to provide for your family:
But if anyone does not provide for his own, and especially for those of his household, he has denied the faith and is worse than an unbeliever.
I Tim 5:8

Determine to be faithful with the little things so that you can be entrusted with more:
If you are faithful in little things, you will be faithful in large ones. But if you are dishonest in little things, you won't be honest with greater responsibilities. And if you are untrustworthy about worldly wealth, who will trust you with the true riches of heaven? And if you are not faithful with other people's things, why should you be trusted with things of your own? **Luke 16:10-12** NLT

Be diligent to leave an inheritance for your children and grandchildren:
Good people leave an inheritance to their grandchildren,
but the sinner's wealth passes to the godly. **Prov 13:22** NLT

Learn to be content with what you have:
Yet true godliness with contentment is itself great wealth. After all, we brought nothing with us when we came into the world, and we can't take anything with us when we leave it. So if we have enough food and clothing, let us be content. **1 Tim 6:6-8** NLT

Recognize that you are blessed to be a blessing:
And it shall come to pass
That just as you were a curse among the nations,
O house of Judah and house of Israel,
So I will save you, and you shall be a blessing.
Do not fear, let your hands be strong. **Zech 8:13**

Work hard at the job you've been given:
He who works his land will have abundant food,
but he who chases fantasies lacks judgment. **Prov 12:11** NIV

Be diligent and disciplined to save over time:
Wealth from get-rich-quick schemes quickly disappears;
wealth from hard work grows over time **Prov 13:11** NLT

Follow the Apostle Paul's example:
I have never coveted anyone's silver or gold or fine clothes. You know that these hands of mine have worked to supply my own needs and even the needs of those who were with me. And I have been a constant example of how you can help those in need by working hard. You should remember the words of the Lord Jesus: "It is more blessed to give than to receive." **Acts 20:33-35** NLT

Remember that God can provide miraculously:
When they had come to Capernaum, those who received the temple tax came to Peter and said, "Does your Teacher not pay the temple tax?"

He said, "Yes."

And when he had come into the house, Jesus anticipated him, saying, "What do you think, Simon? From whom do the kings of the earth take customs or taxes, from their sons or from strangers?"

Peter said to Him, "From strangers."

Jesus said to him, "Then the sons are free. Nevertheless, lest we offend them, go to the sea, cast in a hook, and take the fish that comes up first. And when you have opened its mouth, you will find a piece of money; take that and give it to them for Me and you." **Matt 17:24-27**

A certain woman of the wives of the sons of the prophets cried out to Elisha, saying, "Your servant my husband is dead, and you know that your servant feared the LORD. And the creditor is coming to take my two sons to be his slaves."

So Elisha said to her, "What shall I do for you? Tell me, what do you have in the house?" And she said, "Your maidservant has nothing in the house but a jar of oil."

Then he said, "Go, borrow vessels from everywhere, from all your neighbors—empty vessels; do not gather just a few. And when you have come in, you shall shut the door behind you and your sons; then pour it into all those vessels, and set aside the full ones."

So she went from him and shut the door behind her and her sons, who brought the vessels to her; and she poured it out. Now it came to pass, when the vessels were full, that she said to her son, "Bring me another vessel."

And he said to her, "There is not another vessel." So the oil ceased. Then she came and told the man of God. And he said, "Go, sell the oil and pay your debt; and you and your sons live on the rest." **2 Kings 4:1-7**

Living a Debt-free Life

Seek first the Kingdom of God:
But seek first the kingdom of God and His righteousness, and all these things shall be added to you. Therefore do not worry about tomorrow, for tomorrow will worry about its own things. Sufficient for the day is its own trouble. **Matt 6:33-34**

Be faithful to give your tithes and offerings to the Lord:
"Bring all the tithes into the storehouse so there will be enough food in my Temple. If you do," says the Lord of Heaven's Armies, "I will open the windows of heaven for you. I will pour out a blessing so great you won't have enough room to take it in! Try it! Put me to the test! Your crops will be abundant, for I will guard them from insects and disease. Your grapes will not fall from the vine before they are ripe," says the Lord of Heaven's Armies. "Then all nations will call you blessed, for

your land will be such a delight," says the Lord of Heaven's Armies.
Malachi 3:10-12 NLT

Learn to be content in every situation and learn to draw your strength from Jesus:
Not that I was ever in need, for I have learned how to be content with whatever I have. I know how to live on almost nothing or with everything. I have learned the secret of living in every situation, whether it is with a full stomach or empty, with plenty or little. For I can do everything through Christ, who gives me strength.
Phil 4:11-14 NLT

When blessing comes, do not forget to honor the Lord:
Therefore you shall keep the commandments of the Lord your God, to walk in His ways and to fear Him. For the Lord your God is bringing you into a good land, a land of brooks of water, of fountains and springs, that flow out of valleys and hills; a land of wheat and barley, of vines and fig trees and pomegranates, a land of olive oil and honey; a land in which you will eat bread without scarcity, in which you will lack nothing; a land whose stones are iron and out of whose hills you can dig copper. When you have eaten and are full, then you shall bless the Lord your God for the good land which He has given you.

Beware that you do not forget the Lord your God by not keeping His commandments, His judgments, and His statutes which I command you today, lest—when you have eaten and are full, and have built beautiful houses and dwell in them; and when your herds and your flocks multiply, and your silver and your gold are multiplied, and all that you have is multiplied; when your heart is lifted up, and you forget the Lord your God who brought you out of the land of Egypt, from the house of bondage; who led you through that great and terrible wilderness, in which were fiery serpents and scorpions and thirsty land where there was no water; who brought water for you out of the flinty rock; who fed you in the wilderness with manna, which your fathers did not know, that He might humble you and that He might test you, to do you good in the end—then you say in your heart, "My power and the might of my hand have gained me this wealth."

And you shall remember the Lord your God, for it is He who gives you power to get wealth, that He may establish His covenant which He swore to your fathers, as it is this day. **Deut 8:6-18**

Be faithful to honor your obligations:
Give to everyone what you owe them: Pay your taxes and government fees to those who collect them, and give respect and honor to those who are in authority. **Rom 13:7** NLT

Do your work willingly:
Work willingly at whatever you do, as though you were working for the Lord rather than for people. **Col 3:23** NLT

Do your work for the Lord:
Work with enthusiasm, as though you were working for the Lord rather than for people. **Eph 6:7** NLT

Exercising Your Faith for Financial Breakthrough

So then faith comes by hearing, and hearing by the word of God.
Rom 10:17

Faith is the confidence that what we hope for will actually happen; it gives us assurance about things we cannot see. Through their faith, the people in days of old earned a good reputation.

By faith we understand that the entire universe was formed at God's command, that what we now see did not come from anything that can be seen. **Heb 11:1-3** NLT

And it is impossible to please God without faith. Anyone who wants to come to him must believe that God exists and that he rewards those who sincerely seek him. **Heb 11:6** NLT

Jesus said to him, "If you can believe, all things are possible to him who believes." **Mk 9:23**

He [Jesus] replied, "Because you have so little faith. I tell you the truth, if you have faith as small as a mustard seed, you can say to this mountain, 'Move from here to there' and it will move. Nothing will be impossible for you." **Matt 17:20** NIV

And whatever things you ask in prayer, believing, you will receive." **Matt 21:22**

The thief does not come except to steal, and to kill, and to destroy. I have come that they may have life, and that they may have it more abundantly. **Jn 10:10**

While Jesus was in the Temple, he watched the rich people dropping their gifts in the collection box. Then a poor widow came by and dropped in two small coins. "I tell you the truth," Jesus said, "this poor widow has given more than all the rest of them. For they have given a tiny part of their surplus, but she, poor as she is, has given everything she has." **Luke 21:1-4** NLT

PROCLAIMING GOD'S NAME AND CHARACTER OVER YOUR FINANCES

Speak out these Scripture-based proclamations over your financial situation.
They can also be used in intercession for others. There is power in His name!

You are Jehovah-Jireh, the God who sees my every need and goes before me to provide abundantly. I proclaim Your provision over my every need. **Gen 22:14**

You are Jehovah-Shalom, cause Your peace to reign over every challenge, every place of chaos, attack and unrest in my life and finances. I turn away from anxiety and worry and proclaim that Your peace will guard my heart and mind in Jesus Christ who is my Lord and Savior. **Judges 6:16-24; Phil 4:6-7**

You are Jehovah-M'Kaddesh, the One who sanctifies me. To You, I set apart every aspect of my life: work, home, finances, behavior, thought-life, marriage, children, family, relationships, recreation, ministry and all that You have entrusted to me. I proclaim that You are holy! Purify me that I may live a holy life consecrated to You. **Lev 20:7-8**

You are El Shaddai, God Almighty, my All-Sufficient One. I proclaim that in You, there is more than enough. In You, I have an abundance for everything You have called me to do, plenty for all of my needs and enough to share with others. **Gen 17:1-2; 49:22-26 2 Cor 9:8**

You are my Shepherd, always leading me to green pastures and restoring my soul. I proclaim that in You, I will never be in want. You are my Good Shepherd who has laid down His life for me. I will listen to Your voice. **Ps 23; John 10:11-16**

You are my Father. As the good Abba Father (Daddy) that You are, You will provide for me, protect me and watch over me always. Because I am Your child, I proclaim that I am Your heir and joint-heir with Christ Jesus! **Rom 8:15-17; Matt 6:9-13**

You are Faithful, completely dependable and trustworthy in all that You do. I put my faith in You to fulfill every good promise that You have made to me in Your Word. By Your grace, I commit my life and my finances to Your faithfulness. I ask that You bring health, restoration and increase. I proclaim that I will faithfully use it for Your glory. **Josh 21:45; 1 Cor 1:9; 2 Tim 2:13**

You are my Rock! All of Your deeds are perfect. Everything that You do is just and fair. You are the God of truth and You are without injustice! I proclaim that all of Your ways are righteous and upright. I entrust to You all that concerns me and give my financial situation into Your care. **Deut 32:4**

You are Elohim, the great and mighty God of creation. Lord, You see my situation and all that concerns me. Intervene in Your mighty power and strength and move on my behalf. Attend to every place I have need and bring Your creative provision. I proclaim that You are more than enough! **Gen 1; Ps 35:22-23**

You are Good and all Your ways are good. I proclaim Your perfect goodness, Your lovingkindness and Your mercy in every area of my life. Teach me Your ways so that I will not wander from You. Lord, keep Me always following Your Word. **Ps 119:65-68; Ps 100:5; Jas 1:17**

You are Generous! You have lavished me with Your love, grace and salvation. I proclaim that there is no good thing that You withhold from me as Your child. Create in me Your character of generosity that I may be a blessing to those around me. I purpose to be like You, not giving sparingly or with a bad attitude but joyfully and generously, following Your example. **Eph 1:7-9; Ex 34:5-8; Ps 65:5-13**

You are the God of abundance. I proclaim that in You there is no lack. Lord, I have made Your cause my cause. I have made Your house my house. I have been faithful with the giving of my tithes and offerings and I have been called according to Your name. Now Lord, open the windows of heaven and pour out a flood of blessing, do exceedingly abundantly beyond all that I could ask for or even imagine, for Your glory and renown. **Mal 3:8-12; Eph 3:14-20**

Thirty-One Days of Breakthrough Declarations over Your Finances

Renew your mind about your finances by daily declaring aloud the truth of God's Word.

Day 1:

And the Lord will make you the head and not the tail; you shall be above only, and not be beneath, if you heed the commandments of the Lord your God, which I command you today, and are careful to observe them. **Deut 28:13**

> **Prayer and Declaration:** *Today, Lord Jesus, I set my heart to follow after You, to obey Your commandments and to live by Your Word. I declare Your Word over my life, family, business, and everything that concerns me. You will make me the head and not the tail, I will move ahead and not fall behind. As I follow You faithfully, I declare that You will provide for my every need and lead me out of debt into financial freedom.*

Day 2:

Don't love money; be satisfied with what you have. For God has said, "I will never fail you. I will never abandon you." **Heb 13:5** NLT

> **Prayer and Declaration**: *Forgive me, Lord, for every place in my life where I have given myself to the love of money. I thank You for what You have given to me, I receive it from Your hand with gratefulness. Lord, I declare that You will never fail me and You will never abandon me!*

Day 3:

Wealth gained by dishonesty will be diminished,
But he who gathers by labor will increase. **Prov 13:11**

> **Prayer and Declaration**: *Lord, forgive me for the ways I have tried to gain wealth through any dishonest means. I declare that as I work hard and honor You in all things, You will give growth, increase and blessing.*

Day 4:

If you are faithful in little things, you will be faithful in large ones. But if you are dishonest in little things, you won't be honest with greater responsibilities. And if you are untrustworthy about worldly wealth, who will trust you with the true riches of heaven? And if you are not faithful with other people's things, why should you be trusted with things of your own? No one can serve two masters. For you will hate one and love the other; you will be devoted to one and despise the other. You cannot serve both God and money. **Luke 16:10-13** NLT

> **Prayer and Declaration**: *My Jesus, it is my desire to be a person that You can trust with things no matter if they are small or great. I commit to You today that I will be faithful and honest with the things You have entrusted to me whether it belongs to me or to someone else. I declare today that I am a person of integrity that is trustworthy and who honors You in all that I do. I devote myself to You afresh and will serve only You.*

Day 5:

Wealth and honor come from you alone, for you rule over everything. Power and might are in your hand, and at your discretion people are made great and given strength. **1 Chron 29:12** NLT

> **Prayer and Declaration**: *I recognize today that wealth and honor come from You alone, Ruler of everything! I declare that power and might are in Your hand, and it is You who makes me great and gives me strength.*

Day 6:

If any of you lacks wisdom, let him ask of God, who gives to all liberally and without reproach, and it will be given to him. **James 1:5**

Prayer and Declaration: You are the God of all wisdom and I confess that I need Your wisdom in my life and for my finances. I declare that as I come to You, asking for wisdom, that You will pour it out on me generously without blame or reprimand. I receive Your abundant wisdom and thank You for it!

Day 7:

Watch out! Don't do your good deeds publicly, to be admired by others, for you will lose the reward from your Father in heaven. When you give to someone in need, don't do as the hypocrites do—blowing trumpets in the synagogues and streets to call attention to their acts of charity! I tell you the truth, they have received all the reward they will ever get. But when you give to someone in need, don't let your left hand know what your right hand is doing. Give your gifts in private, and your Father, who sees everything, will reward you. **Matt 6:1-4** NLT

Prayer and Declaration: Lord, I thank You for all that You have given to me. Would You show me to whom I am to be a blessing today? I want to honor You by giving to those in need and I will do it quietly because I know that You are El Roi, the God who sees. I declare today that I am available to You to bless others through me at any time and as I give in private, my reward will come from You.

Day 8:

Honor the Lord with your wealth
and with the best part of everything you produce. **Prov 3:9** NLT

Prayer and Declaration: It is my desire to give to You from the very best of everything I have and everything that I produce. I declare that I will be a person of excellence. I will give to You the best that I am and the best that I have!

Day 9:

Give to everyone what you owe them: Pay your taxes and government fees to those who collect them, and give respect and honor to those who are in authority. **Rom 13:7** NLT

> **Prayer and Declaration**: *Lord, I ask Your forgiveness for the debt that I have gotten myself into and I declare and make it my purpose to payback responsibly all that I owe to others. Forgive me for the ways that I have dishonored those in authority over me, including those in governmental positions. From now on, I will be a person of honor in everything that I do and I will show respect to those who are in authority.*

Day 10:

Remember this—a farmer who plants only a few seeds will get a small crop. But the one who plants generously will get a generous crop. You must each decide in your heart how much to give. And don't give reluctantly or in response to pressure. "For God loves a person who gives cheerfully." And God will generously provide all you need. Then you will always have everything you need and plenty left over to share with others. As the Scriptures say,

"They share freely and give generously to the poor.
Their good deeds will be remembered forever."

For God is the one who provides seed for the farmer and then bread to eat. In the same way, he will provide and increase your resources and then produce a great harvest of generosity in you.

Yes, you will be enriched in every way so that you can always be generous. **2 Cor 9:6-11** NLT

> **Prayer and Declaration**: *Generosity is not just what You do but it is who You are! I want to be just like You, Lord. I want to be a joyful*

and abundant giver, not because I have to but because I get to be a blessing to others! I declare that as I give generously and with joy that You will produce a harvest of generosity in me so that I can increase even more in my giving.

Day 11:

But people who long to be rich fall into temptation and are trapped by many foolish and harmful desires that plunge them into ruin and destruction. For the love of money is the root of all kinds of evil. And some people, craving money, have wandered from the true faith and pierced themselves with many sorrows.
1 Tim 6:9-10 NLT

> **Prayer and Declaration**: *Cleanse me, my Savior, of the love of money. I want my heart to be free and my motives toward money to be purified. Lord, keep me from ruin and destruction. Please break off every craving for money and riches from me. I declare that my heart is free to be entrusted with wealth so that I can honor You with it. My heart and my finances belong wholly to You.*

Day 12:

If you are a thief, quit stealing. Instead, use your hands for good hard work, and then give generously to others in need. **Eph 4:28** NLT

> **Prayer and Declaration**: *I ask You to forgive me, Lord, for stealing. (If the Holy Spirit brings any specific instances of stealing to mind, confess that to Him specifically and ask Jesus to forgive you. If it is in your power to make restitution, give back what you have stolen, make every effort to do so.) Today, I declare that I will live my life with honesty and integrity. I will be a hard worker at everything I am given to do so that I can bless others generously.*

Day 13:

Choose a good reputation over great riches;
being held in high esteem is better than silver or gold. **Prov 22:1** NLT

> **Prayer and Declaration**: *Today, my Lord, I choose a good reputation over riches. I declare that I will seek to live my life so that favor and a good reputation will be the fruit that is produced.*

Day 14:

Good people leave an inheritance to their grandchildren,
but the sinner's wealth passes to the godly. **Prov 13:22** NLT

> **Prayer and Declaration**: *I ask You, Abba Father, that You would give me the wisdom, favor and diligence to provide well for my family. I declare that I will work hard and save faithfully to leave behind an inheritance, not only for my children, but also for my grandchildren.*

Day 15:

But remember the Lord your God, for it is he who gives you the ability to produce wealth, and so confirms his covenant, which he swore to your forefathers, as it is today. **Deut 8:18** NIV

> **Prayer and Declaration**: *You are the Lord my God! I ask that You give me the ability to produce wealth. I declare that as Your son or daughter through Jesus Christ, I am grafted into Your covenant and I gratefully receive the fullness of that matchless inheritance (Rom 8:17).*

Day 16:

In the house of the wise are stores of choice food and oil,
but a foolish man devours all he has. **Prov 21:20** NIV

Prayer and Declaration: *Lord Jesus, I thank You for the lesson in this verse. I determine today to make my home a house of the wise. As Your son or daughter, I want no part of a poverty mindset that devours everything that I get. I ask You to break off every aspect of mindset that is at work in my life and finances. Today, I declare that I am a child of God and I dedicate my life and home to the wisdom of the Lord. I will be a wise steward of all that is entrusted to me.*

Day 17:

Yet true godliness with contentment is itself great wealth. After all, we brought nothing with us when we came into the world, and we can't take anything with us when we leave it. So if we have enough food and clothing, let us be content. **I Tim 6:6-8** NLT

Prayer and Declaration: *It is true, my Lord, that I brought nothing with me when I came into this world. All that I have comes from You. I ask that You teach me to be content. I look to You to provide enough of the things that I need for daily life. I declare that I will be grateful and content with what I have been given.*

Day 18:

Praise the Lord!
How joyful are those who fear the Lord
and delight in obeying his commands.
Their children will be successful everywhere;
an entire generation of godly people will be blessed.
They themselves will be wealthy,
and their good deeds will last forever.
Light shines in the darkness for the godly.
They are generous, compassionate, and righteous.
Good comes to those who lend money generously
and conduct their business fairly. **Ps 112:1-5** NLT

Prayer and Declaration: *Jehovah-Jireh, You are my provider! I find joy and delight in following Your ways by living a life of generosity, compassion and righteousness in Christ Jesus. I declare that my children will be blessed and successful. I commit the wealth that You have given to me to be used for Your purposes. I will seek to conduct my business fairly and with integrity.*

Day 19:

Trust in the Lord and do good.
Then you will live safely in the land and prosper.
Take delight in the Lord,
and he will give you your heart's desires.
Commit everything you do to the Lord.
Trust him, and he will help you.
He will make your innocence radiate like the dawn,
and the justice of your cause will shine like the noonday sun.
Ps 37:3-6 NLT

Prayer and Declaration: *I trust in You, Lord. Teach me what it means to delight in You and to live my life committing everything to You. I trust in You and thank You for helping me. As I truly delight in You, I trust You to give me the desires of my heart. One of my desires, Lord, is to live a debt-free life! I declare that You are wholly trustworthy and that the justice of my cause will shine like the noonday sun!*

Day 20:

Do you see a man who excels in his work?
He will stand before kings;
He will not stand before unknown men. **Prov 22:29**

Prayer and Declaration: *Lord, it is my desire to be a person of excellence that excels in the work You have given me to do. I*

*declare that as I work hard and conduct my work with integrity that
You will make a way for me to stand with favor before people of
authority and power. Make a way for me, Lord, so that I do not live
in obscurity but rather I can be a person of influence for Your glory.*

Day 21:

Wisdom is the principal thing;
Therefore get wisdom.
And in all your getting, get understanding.
Exalt her, and she will promote you;
She will bring you honor, when you embrace her.
She will place on your head an ornament of grace;
A crown of glory she will deliver to you. **Prov 4:7-9**

> **Prayer and Declaration**: *You are the source of true wisdom, Lord.
> I come to You asking for an increase of wisdom in every aspect
> of my life. I purpose today to seek after wisdom and to learn
> how to apply it in practical matters. I declare that as I become a
> person of wisdom and good judgement, You will promote me and
> honor me. You will cause grace to rest on me like an ornament or
> garland.*

Day 22:

Tainted wealth has no lasting value,
but right living can save your life.
The Lord will not let the godly go hungry,
but he refuses to satisfy the craving of the wicked.
Lazy people are soon poor;
hard workers get rich.
The blessing of the Lord makes a person rich,
And He adds no sorrow with it. **Prov 10:2-4, 22** NLT

Prayer and Declaration: *I dedicate myself to You in a fresh way today, my Lord. I deeply desire to live according to Your ways, to be a godly person who works hard and enjoys Your blessing. I declare that it is Your blessing that makes me rich.*

Day 23:

Better a little with the fear of the Lord
than great wealth with turmoil. **Prov 15:16** NIV

Prayer and Declaration: *I live in awe and reverence of You, my God. I thank You for what I have whether small or great. I declare that it is far better to live with the good that You have given to me than to live in turmoil and trouble.*

Day 24:

So don't worry about these things, saying, "What will we eat? What will we drink? What will we wear?" These things dominate the thoughts of unbelievers, but your heavenly Father already knows all your needs. Seek the Kingdom of God above all else, and live righteously, and he will give you everything you need. So don't worry about tomorrow, for tomorrow will bring its own worries. Today's trouble is enough for today. **Matt 6:31-34** NLT

Prayer and Declaration: *Lord, increase my faith today to trust You to meet all of my needs. I want my thoughts to be dominated with Your thoughts and my life with seeking first Your Kingdom. Teach me, Lord, how to be mindful of my thoughts so that I do not live in worry about tomorrow. I declare that I will intentionally live in the moment, trusting You to provide all that I need today.*

Day 25:

I [Wisdom] love all who love me.
Those who search will surely find me.

I have riches and honor,
as well as enduring wealth and justice.
My gifts are better than gold, even the purest gold,
my wages better than sterling silver!
I walk in righteousness,
in paths of justice.
Those who love me inherit wealth.
I will fill their treasuries. **Prov 8:17-21** NLT

> **Prayer and Declaration**: *Lord, I want to be one who truly loves and lives in wisdom. I declare that wisdom is more valuable than any earthly treasure! I will walk in wisdom's righteousness and paths of justice!*

Day 26:

Then David praised the Lord in the presence of the whole assembly:

"O Lord, the God of our ancestor Israel, may you be praised forever and ever! Yours, O Lord, is the greatness, the power, the glory, the victory, and the majesty. Everything in the heavens and on earth is yours, O Lord, and this is your kingdom. We adore you as the one who is over all things. Wealth and honor come from you alone, for you rule over everything. Power and might are in your hand, and at your discretion people are made great and given strength. O our God, we thank you and praise your glorious name! But who am I, and who are my people, that we could give anything to you? Everything we have has come from you, and we give you only what you first gave us!" **I Chron 29:10-14** NLT

> **Prayer and Declaration**: *I worship You, Giver of all that is good! Lord, I stand in awe of who You are and I praise Your glorious name. Like David, I am humbled that You would allow me to give to You. What an honor and privilege. Lord, I declare that I will be a faithful*

giver. I dedicate afresh to You all that I have and all that I am,
knowing that all things come from You.

Day 27:

There should be no poor among you, for the Lord your God will greatly bless you in the land he is giving you as a special possession. You will receive this blessing if you are careful to obey all the commands of the Lord your God that I am giving you today. The Lord your God will bless you as he has promised. You will lend money to many nations but will never need to borrow. You will rule many nations, but they will not rule over you. **Deut 15:4-6** NLT

> **Prayer and Declaration**: *I thank You for grafting me into the promises You gave to Israel, through the death and resurrection of Jesus. I declare today that I am Your child and Jesus' righteousness is my righteousness. I, therefore, receive the fullness of Your blessing even as You promised!*

Day 28:

Teach those who are rich in this world not to be proud and not to trust in their money, which is so unreliable. Their trust should be in God, who richly gives us all we need for our enjoyment. **1 Tim 6:17** NLT

> **Prayer and Declaration**: *Forgive me, Lord, for any pride in my heart about the abundance that I have and for putting my trust in it. I recognize that riches can be so unreliable and uncertain. I declare that I will trust in You, God, for You are completely reliable. You have abundantly provided all things for my enjoyment.*

Day 29:

The wicked borrows and does not repay,
But the righteous shows mercy and gives. **Ps 37:21**

Prayer and Declaration: *I commit myself, my Lord, to diligently repay all that I owe to others. I ask that You enable me to live a debt free life according to Your ways! I declare that I will be a righteous person who shows mercy and gives generously to others.*

Day 30:

Do not lay up for yourselves treasures on earth, where moth and rust destroy and where thieves break in and steal; but lay up for yourselves treasures in heaven, where neither moth nor rust destroys and where thieves do not break in and steal. For where your treasure is, there your heart will be also. **Matt 6:19-21**

Prayer and Declaration: *Lord Jesus, You are my true treasure! Your gift of eternal life is more valuable than any riches this earth has to offer. I declare that my treasure is You, Jesus, and my heart is set fully on You!*

Day 31:

And my God shall supply all your need according to His riches in glory by Christ Jesus. **Phil 4:19**

Prayer and Declaration: *You, precious Jesus, are my God. I declare that in Christ all of my needs are generously met according to Your riches in glory! I declare that by Your grace, I will live a life of freedom from debt. As I begin to practically apply the keys that You have given me in Your Word, lead me into a season of turnaround! I declare that by Your wisdom, I will live a life of abundance for Your glory!*